PRAYING THE WORD

Praying the Word

Illuminated Prayers and Wisdom from
The Saint John's Bible

Donald Jackson — Artistic Director
The Saint John's Bible
Collegeville, Minnesota

A Saint John's Bible Book
published by
Liturgical Press
Collegeville, Minnesota

www.saintjohnsbible.org

Library of Congress Cataloging-in-
Publication Data

Bible. English. New Revised Standard.
Selections. 2008.
  Praying the word : illuminated prayers
and wisdom from the Saint John's Bible /
Donald Jackson.
      p. cm.
  ISBN 978-0-8146-9093-2 (hardcover)
1. Bible—Devotional use. 2. Bible—
Illustrations. I. Jackson, Donald, 1938-
II. Title.
  BS391.3.J33 2008
  220.5'20436—dc22
                    2008011799

Contents

Introduction	6
Psalm 1	8
The Alien Who Resides with You	10
The Lord Bless You	12
Hear, O Israel—Deuteronomy	14
I Call Heaven and Earth	16
Psalm 23	18
Make Yourselves Clean	20
He Shall Judge Between the Nations	22
Comfort, O Comfort My People	24
Listen to Me, O Coastlands	26
Arise, Shine	28
Now the Word of the Lord	30
Do Justice, Love Kindness, Walk Humbly	32
Psalm 42	34
I Am My Beloved's	36
Set Me as a Seal upon Your Heart	38
Wisdom Is Radiant	40
To Fear the Lord Is the Fullness of Wisdom	42
Faithful Friends	44
Like Clay in the Hand of the Potter	46
She Is a Reflection	48
Psalm 63	50
Beatitudes	52
Lord's Prayer	54
You Shall Love the Lord—Matthew	56
Hear, O Israel—Mark	58
Canticle of Mary	60
Canticle of Zechariah	62
Canticle of Simeon	66
You Shall Love the Lord—Luke	68
Those Who Believe in Me	70
Repent and Be Baptized	72
Psalm 150	74
Credits	76

Saint Benedict writes in his Holy Rule, "So that in all things God may be glorified." God's glorification is the object of every good work, thought, and deed. No wonder, then, that a prayer book would fuse these three human acts. They count for perfect prayer, and among many things and in the best of all moments, these works, thoughts, and deeds yield great art.

The association of art with prayer has a long history within the Christian tradition. From the frescoes on catacomb walls to countless chapels and churches throughout the world, art is as present as the kneeler. Art has left a noble legacy in Christian prayer books as well. We can think of the great lectionaries and sacramentaries used in churches and cathedrals for public worship, or the many Psalters in the hands of chanting monks and nuns within their cloisters. Nobles such as the Duc de Berry and Count Farnese commissioned small but exquisite Books of Hours for their own use. The prayer book you now hold, a work inspired by *The Saint John's Bible*, stands in this great tradition of the book arts.

Associating art with prayer in the Christian tradition owes its birth to the Incarnation, for the Incarnation is the foundation of all things Christian. God takes on human flesh in the person of Jesus Christ, and all creation is blessed with his grace. If all creation is sanctified through Christ, how much more so the person at prayer. The daily and sacred conversation we call prayer transforms us into the divine likeness.

Using text illuminations from the Pentateuch, Psalms, Prophets, Wisdom Books, and the New Testament, this prayer book combines the Word of Sacred Scripture with the beauty of sacred art. It is designed to be prayed slowly and meditatively in the manner of the Benedictine practice of *lectio divina*. *Lectio divina*, a Latin term meaning "sacred reading," necessitates a quiet and peaceful time and place for one to read and reread a small section of Scripture. Furthermore, this book is designed to promote *visio divina*, or "sacred viewing." If we are meant to reread a passage meditatively, we are also called to view and review an image. The two practices work in tandem to bring one into the presence of God.

Some of the biblical readings within the prayer book will be intimately familiar from their use in the liturgy and personal devotions. All of the readings richly reflect the history of salvation as understood by Christians. Each selection, familiar or not, calls us to read and view again and again so that, in the process, the Holy Spirit can enkindle within us the fire of love. And thus in all things God may be glorified.

Michael Patella, OSB

Chair of *The Saint John's Bible* Committee on Illumination and Text

This wisdom psalm teaches that the pathway to upright living requires daily meditation on the teaching of the Lord, particularly that which is communicated through the following 149 psalms of the Psalter.

Psalm 1

Happy are those
    who do not follow the advice of the wicked,
or take the path that sinners tread,
    or sit in the seat of scoffers;
2 but their delight is in the law of the LORD,
    and on his law they meditate day and night.
3 They are like trees
    planted by streams of water,
which yield their fruit in its season,
    and their leaves do not wither.
In all that they do, they prosper.

4 The wicked are not so,
    but are like chaff that the wind drives away.
5 Therefore the wicked will not stand
        in the judgment,
    nor sinners in the congregation
        of the righteous;
6 for the LORD watches over the way
        of the righteous,
    but the way of the wicked will perish.

THE ALIEN WHO RESIDES WITH YOU

Leviticus 19:34

This ethical commandment from the Holiness Code demands that foreigners who respect the Israelite tradition be granted hospitality in the land of Israel.

THE ALIEN *who resides with you*
shall be to you as the citizen among
you; you shall love the alien as yourself,
for you were aliens in the land of Egypt:
I am the LORD *your God.*

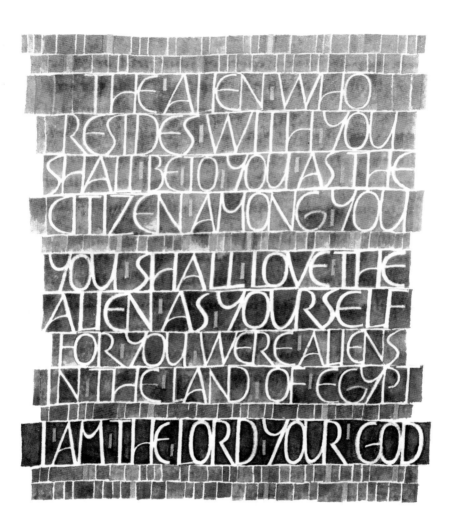

THE ALIEN WHO
RESIDES WITH YOU
SHALL BE TO YOU AS THE
CITIZEN AMONG YOU
YOU SHALL LOVE THE
ALIEN AS YOURSELF
FOR YOU WERE ALIENS
IN THE LAND OF EGYPT
I AM THE LORD YOUR GOD

The Lord Bless You

Numbers 6:24-26

Known as the "Aaronic Blessing," this priestly blessing calls forth the Lord's protection by describing the Lord's presence as life-giving light.

THE LORD
BLESS YOU
AND KEEP YOU;
THE LORD MAKE
HIS FACE TO SHINE
UPON YOU, AND
BE GRACIOUS
TO YOU;
THE LORD
LIFT UP HIS
COUNTENANCE
UPON YOU,
AND GIVE YOU
PEACE.

Deuteronomy 6:4-5

The Shema, the essential prayer of Judaism, proclaims the uniqueness of the Lord God. Jesus also says the same prayer in chapter 12 of Mark's gospel.

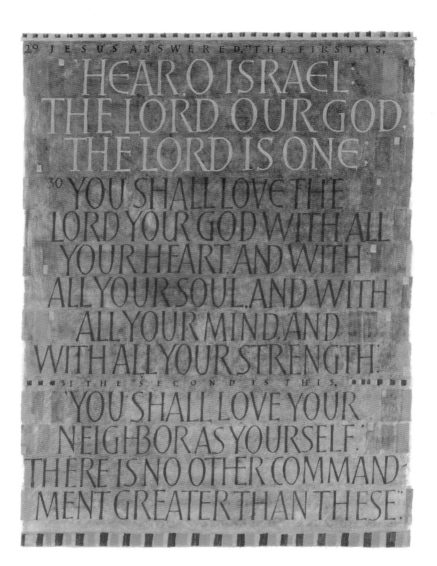

"HEAR, O ISRAEL:
THE LORD OUR GOD,
THE LORD IS ONE;
30 'YOU SHALL LOVE THE
LORD YOUR GOD WITH ALL
YOUR HEART, AND WITH
ALL YOUR SOUL, AND WITH
ALL YOUR MIND, AND
WITH ALL YOUR STRENGTH.'
31 THE SECOND IS THIS,
'YOU SHALL LOVE YOUR
NEIGHBOR AS YOURSELF.'
THERE IS NO OTHER COMMAND-
MENT GREATER THAN THESE."

I Call Heaven and Earth

Deuteronomy 30:19-20

This directive within a covenant ceremony emphasizes that when individuals decide to commit themselves to the Lord it impacts the community through the generations.

I CALL *heaven and earth to witness*
against you today that I have set before
you life and death, blessings and curses.
Choose life so that you and your descen-
dants may live, loving the LORD your
God, obeying him, and holding fast
to him; for that means life to you and
length of days, so that you may live in
the land that the LORD swore to give to
your ancestors, to Abraham, to Isaac,
and to Jacob.

This psalm of confidence in the midst of trying circumstances expresses firm hope that the Lord will protect and bless those who turn to him. This psalm has traditionally been a strong source of consolation at the time of the loss of a loved one.

Psalm 23

A Psalm of David.

The LORD is my shepherd, I shall not want.
2   He makes me lie down in green pastures;
he leads me beside still waters;
3   he restores my soul.
He leads me in right paths
for his name's sake.

4 Even though I walk through
the darkest valley,
I fear no evil;
for you are with me;
your rod and your staff—
they comfort me.

5 You prepare a table before me
in the presence of my enemies;
you anoint my head with oil;
my cup overflows.
6 Surely goodness and mercy shall follow me
all the days of my life,
and I shall dwell in the house of the LORD
my whole life long.

Make Yourselves Clean

These passages command the people of Jerusalem to purify themselves and to carry out social justice; they are the concluding part of an instruction on proper worship of the Lord.

Wash yourselves
make yourselves clean
remove the evil of your doings
from before my eyes

CEASE·TO·DO·EVIL·
LEARN·TO·DO·GOOD·
SEEK·JUSTICE·
·RESCUE·THE·OPPRESSED·
·DEFEND·THE·ORPHAN·
·PLEAD·FOR·THE·WIDOW·

He Shall Judge Between the Nations

Isaiah 2:4

This concluding statement of Isaiah's announcement of the nations streaming toward Jerusalem for instruction (2:2-4) promises that peace will come among nations when they recognize the sovereignty of the Lord.

He shall judge
between the nations
and shall arbitrate
for many peoples

they shall beat their
swords into plowshares
and their spears
into pruning hooks

NATION·SHALL·NOT·LIFT·UP·
·SWORD·AGAINST·NATION·
·NEITHER·SHALL·THEY·
·LEARN·WAR·ANY·MORE·

COMFORT, O COMFORT MY PEOPLE

Isaiah 40:1-5

From the opening speech addressed to the Babylonian exiles (Isaiah 40–55), this message of salvation and hope announces a new exodus in which the Israelites and all the nations will witness the glory of the Lord upon Israel's return to its homeland.

Comfort · O comfort my people
says your God
Speak tenderly to Jerusalem
and cry to her
that she has served her term
that her penalty is paid
that she has received
from the LORD's hand
double for all her sins

· 回 ·

A voice cries out ·
In the wilderness
prepare the way of the LORD
make straight in the desert
a highway for our God
Every valley shall be lifted up
and every mountain & hill
be made low
the uneven ground
shall become level
and the rough places a plain
Then the glory of the LORD
shall be revealed
and all people shall see it together
for the mouth of
the LORD has spoken

Listen to Me, O Coastlands

Isaiah 49:1-4

This introductory section from the second of the four Servant Songs (42:1-7; 49:1-7; 50:4-9; 52:13–53:12) emphasizes Israel's status as a chosen people whose trials bring light to the nations.

Listen to me
O coastlands
pay attention you peoples
from far away! The LORD
called me before I was born
while I was in my
mother's womb he named me
He made my mouth like
a sharp sword in the shadow
of his hand he hid me he
made me a polished arrow
in his quiver he hid
me away And he said
to me you are my servant,
Israel, in whom I will be
glorified But I said I have
labored in vain I have
spent my strength
for nothing and vanity
Yet surely my cause is
with the LORD and my
reward with my God

Arise, Shine

This announcement of salvation to the Israelites whose homeland had been devastated aims to lift their sights toward the glorious deeds that the Lord is about to do for them. The glory of the Lord will encompass the Israelites and draw all the nations toward Jerusalem.

ARISE·SHINE
FOR·YOUR·LIGHT·HAS·COME
AND·THE·GLORY·OF·THE·LORD
HAS·RISEN·UPON·YOU

For·darkness·shall·cover·the·earth·
and·thick·darkness·the·peoples·
but·the·LORD·will·arise·upon·you·
and·his·glory·will·appear·over·you

NATIONS·SHALL·COME
TO·YOUR·LIGHT·AND
KINGS·TO·THE·BRIGHTNESS
OF·YOUR·DAWN

NOW THE WORD OF THE LORD

Jeremiah 1:4-10

Jeremiah was called at a young age to be a prophet to the nations. The Lord commissioned him to speak words of judgment that would tear down nations and words of salvation that would re-build them.

NOW THE WORD *of the* LORD *came to me saying,*
    "Before I formed you in the womb I knew you,
    and before you were born I consecrated you;
    I appointed you a prophet to the nations."
Then I said, "Ah, Lord GOD! *Truly I do not know how to speak, for I am only a boy."*
But the LORD *said to me,*
    "Do not say, 'I am only a boy';
    for you shall go to all to whom I send you,
    and you shall speak whatever I command you,
    Do not be afraid of them,
    for I am with you to deliver you, says the LORD."
Then the LORD *put out his hand and touched my mouth; and the* LORD *said to me,*
    "Now I have put my words in your mouth.
    See, today I appoint you over nations and over kingdoms,
    to pluck up and to pull down,
    to destroy and to overthrow,
    to build and to plant."

NOW THE WORD
OF THE LORD CAME
TO ME SAYING

THEN I SAID: AH LORD
GOD TRULY I DO NOT
KNOW HOW TO SPEAK
FOR I AM ONLY A BOY
BUT THE LORD SAID TO ME

THEN THE LORD PUT OUT
HIS HAND AND TOUCHED
MY MOUTH AND THE
LORD SAID TO ME

Do Justice, Love Kindness, Walk Humbly

Micah 6:8

This prophetic pronouncement declares ethical behavior to be more important than sacrificial offerings. It concludes a passage (6:6-8) that reflects a liturgy at the entrance to a sanctuary, a ritual action that finds a Christian analog in the penitential rite of the eucharistic liturgy.

He has told you
O mortal
what is good

---

and what does
the LORD require of you
but to do justice
and to love kindness
& to walk humbly
with your God

PSALM 42

This lament psalm provides the troubled believer with the words needed to express a painful experience of God's absence and to implore God to return. The water imagery emphasizes the need for God's constant presence so that one's spiritual thirst can be slaked and the chaotic flood waters of life can be navigated.

Psalm 42

To the leader. A Maskil of the Korahites.

As a deer longs for flowing streams,
   so my soul longs for you, O God.
2 My soul thirsts for God,
   for the living God.
When shall I come and behold
   the face of God?
3 My tears have been my food
   day and night,
while people say to me continually,
   "Where is your God?"

4 These things I remember,
   as I pour out my soul:
how I went with the throng,
   and led them in procession to
      the house of God,
with glad shouts and songs of thanksgiving,
   a multitude keeping festival.
5 Why are you cast down, O my soul,
   and why are you disquieted within me?
Hope in God; for I shall again praise him,
   my help 6 and my God.

My soul is cast down within me;
   therefore I remember you
from the land of Jordan and of Hermon,
   from Mount Mizar.
7 Deep calls to deep
   at the thunder of your cataracts;
all your waves and your billows
   have gone over me.
8 By day the LORD commands his steadfast love,
   and at night his song is with me,
   a prayer to the God of my life.

9 I say to God, my rock,
   "Why have you forgotten me?
Why must I walk about mournfully
   because the enemy oppresses me?"
10 As with a deadly wound in my body,
   my adversaries taunt me,
while they say to me continually,
   "Where is your God?"

11 Why are you cast down, O my soul,
   and why are you disquieted within me?
Hope in God; for I shall again praise him,
   my help and my God.

I Am My Beloved's

Song of Solomon 6:3

This dialogue, in which a woman is the main speaker, highlights the woman's love for her beloved. Saint Bernard identifies the lover with the individual believer and the beloved as Christ.

I AM MY BELOVED'S &
MY BELOVED IS MINE
HE PASTURES HIS FLOCK
AMONG THE LILIES

Set Me as a Seal upon Your Heart

Song of Solomon 8:6-7

Here the lover is aflame with an overwhelming desire to be united with the beloved. This profound experience of human love can also be part of the believer's relationship with God. Origen identifies the beloved with Christ and the lover with the church or the individual believer.

Set me as a seal *upon your heart,*
 as a seal upon your arm;
for love is strong as death,
 passion fierce as the grave.
Its flashes are flashes of fire,
 a raging flame.
Many waters cannot quench love,
 neither can floods drown it.
If one offered for love
 all the wealth of one's house,
 it would be utterly scorned.

SET ME AS A SEAL
UPON YOUR HEART
AS A SEAL UPON
YOUR ARM
FOR LOVE IS
STRONG AS DEATH
PASSION FIERCE
AS THE GRAVE
ITS FLASHES ARE
FLASHES OF FIRE
A RAGING FLAME
MANY WATERS CAN
NOT QUENCH LOVE
NEITHER CAN
FLOODS DROWN IT
IF ONE OFFERED
FOR LOVE
ALL THE WEALTH
OF ONES HOUSE
IT WOULD BE
UTTERLY SCORNED

Wisdom Is Radiant

Wisdom 6:12-18

A personification of a function of God, Woman Wisdom is an active presence who embraces and enlightens those who desire her. She accompanies those who seek God and strengthens them in their obedient listening and careful reflection.

Wisdom is radiant *and unfading,*
and she is easily discerned by those who love her,
and is found by those who seek her.
She hastens to make herself known to those who desire her.
One who rises early to seek her will have no difficulty,
for she will be found sitting at the gate.
To fix one's thought on her is perfect understanding,
and one who is vigilant on her account will soon be free from care,
because she goes about seeking those worthy of her,
and she graciously appears to them in their paths,
and meets them in every thought.

Wisdom is radiant and unfading, and she is easily discerned by those who love her, and is found by those who seek her. She hastens to make herself known to those who desire her. One who rises early to seek her will have no difficulty, for she will be found sitting at the gate. To fix one's thought on her is perfect understanding, and one who is vigilant on her account will soon be free from care, because she goes about seeking those worthy of her, and she graciously appears to them in their paths, and meets them in every thought.

To Fear the Lord Is the Fullness of Wisdom

Sirach 1:16-17

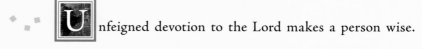nfeigned devotion to the Lord makes a person wise. Those who revere the Lord are blessed abundantly with the presence of Woman Wisdom.

To
fear the
Lord is
fullness of
wisdom
she
inebriates
mortals with
her fruits
she
fills their
whole house
with
desirable
goods
and their
storehouses
with her
produce

Faithful Friends

Sirach 6:14-22

Friends are an invaluable gift from God. Those who seek the friendship of Woman Wisdom accept the discipline necessary to receive her, for she will guide them in the ways of love.

Faithful friends *are a sturdy shelter:*
  whoever finds one has found a treasure.
Faithful friends are beyond price;
  no amount can balance their worth.
Faithful friends are life-saving medicine;
  and those who fear the Lord will find them.
Those who fear the Lord direct their friendship aright,
  for as they are, so are their neighbors also.

My child, from your youth choose discipline,
  and when you have gray hair you will still find wisdom.
Come to her like one who plows and sows,
  and wait for her good harvest.
For when you cultivate her you will toil but little,
  and soon you will eat of her produce.
She seems very harsh to the undisciplined;
  fools cannot remain with her.
She will be like a heavy stone to test them,
  and they will not delay in casting her aside.
For wisdom is like her name;
  she is not readily perceived by many.

Faithful friends are a sturdy
shelter: whoever finds one has
found a treasure. Faithful
friends are beyond price; no
amount can balance their worth.
Faithful friends are life-saving
medicine; and those who fear
the Lord will find them. Those
who fear the Lord direct their
friendship aright, for as they
are, so are their neighbors also.

My child, from your youth
choose discipline, and when
you have gray hair you will
still find wisdom.
Come to her like one who plows
and sows, and wait for her good
harvest. For when you cultivate
her you will toil but little, and
soon you will eat of her produce.
She seems very harsh to the
undisciplined; fools cannot
remain with her. She will be
like a heavy stone to test them,
and they will not delay in
casting her aside.

For wisdom
is like her name;
she is not readily
perceived by many.

Like Clay in the Hand of the Potter

Sirach 33:13

God is the One who shapes the diverse destinies of all parts of creation. The wise person is attentive to this divine order within society and nature because obedience to God brings life.

LIKE CLAY IN THE HAND OF THE POTTER, TO BE MOLDED AS HE PLEASES, SO ALL ARE IN THE HAND OF THEIR MAKER, TO BE GIVEN WHATEVER HE DECIDES

SHE IS A REFLECTION

Wisdom 7:26

God's active presence in humans and all of creation is personified in the absolute perfection of Woman Wisdom. Her origin even transcends the immaterial reality of eternal light.

she
is a
reflection
of
eternal
light.
a
spotless
mirror
of the
working
of
God.

and
an
image
of
his
goodness

An ardent longing for God is a sign of a growing, vital life of prayer. This psalm promises those who yearn for God the comfort and assurance of God's presence and protection.

Psalm 63

A Psalm of David, when he was in the
Wilderness of Judah.

O God, you are my God, I seek you,
 my soul thirsts for you;
my flesh faints for you,
 as in a dry and weary land
 where there is no water.
2 So I have looked upon you in the sanctuary,
 beholding your power and glory.
3 Because your steadfast love is better than life,
 my lips will praise you.
4 So I will bless you as long as I live;
 I will lift up my hands and call on your name.

5 My soul is satisfied as with a rich feast,
 and my mouth praises you with joyful lips
6 when I think of you on my bed,
 and meditate on you in the watches
 of the night;
7 for you have been my help,
 and in the shadow of your wings
 I sing for joy.
8 My soul clings to you;
 your right hand upholds me.

9 But those who seek to destroy my life
 shall go down into the depths of the earth;
10 they shall be given over to the power
 of the sword,
 they shall be prey for jackals.
11 But the king shall rejoice in God;
 all who swear by him shall exult,
 for the mouths of liars will be stopped.

Beatitudes

Matthew 5:3-12

s instruction proclaimed from a mountain, Matthew's Beatitudes parallel Moses receiving the Law on Mount Sinai.

Blessed are *the poor in spirit,*
for theirs is the kingdom of heaven.
Blessed are those who mourn,
for they will be comforted.
Blessed are the meek,
for they will inherit the earth.
Blessed are those who hunger and thirst for righteousness,
for they will be filled.
Blessed are the merciful,
for they will receive mercy.
Blessed are the pure in heart,
for they will see God.
Blessed are the peacemakers,
for they will be called children of God.
Blessed are those who are persecuted for righteousness' sake,
for theirs is the kingdom of heaven.
Blessed are you when people revile you and persecute you and utter all kinds of evil against you falsely on my account. Rejoice and be glad, for your reward is great in heaven, for in the same way they persecuted the prophets who were before you.

BLESSED ARE THE POOR IN SPIRIT FOR
THEIRS IS THE KINGDOM OF HEAVEN
BLESSED ARE THOSE WHO MOURN
FOR THEY WILL BE COMFORTED
BLESSED ARE THE MEEK FOR
THEY WILL INHERIT THE EARTH
BLESSED ARE THOSE WHO HUNGER
AND THIRST FOR RIGHTEOUSNESS
FOR THEY WILL BE FILLED
BLESSED ARE THE MERCIFUL
FOR THEY WILL RECEIVE MERCY
BLESSED ARE THE PURE IN
HEART FOR THEY WILL SEE GOD
BLESSED ARE THE PEACEMAKERS FOR
THEY WILL BE CALLED CHILDREN OF GOD
BLESSED ARE THOSE WHO ARE PERSE
CUTED FOR RIGHTEOUSNESS SAKE FOR
THEIRS IS THE KINGDOM OF HEAVEN
BLESSED ARE YOU WHEN PEOPLE REVILE
YOU AND PERSECUTE YOU AND UTTER
ALL KINDS OF EVIL AGAINST YOU
FALSELY ON MY ACCOUNT REJOICE AND BE
GLAD FOR YOUR REWARD IS GREAT IN HEAVEN
FOR IN THE SAME WAY THEY
PERSECUTED THE PROPHETS WHO
WERE BEFORE YOU

LORD'S PRAYER

Matthew 6:9-13

Because Christ himself taught his disciples this prayer, it occupies a special place in the heart of Christians. The prayer combines the needs of this world with the promises of the world to come.

OUR FATHER *in heaven,*
> *hallowed be your name.*
> *Your kingdom come.*
> *Your will be done,*
>> *on earth as it is in heaven.*
> *Give us this day our daily bread.*
> *And forgive us our debts,*
>> *as we also have forgiven our debtors.*
> *And do not bring us to the time of trial,*
>> *but rescue us from the evil one.*

Our Father in heaven,
hallowed be your name.
Your kingdom come.
Your will be done.
on earth as it is in heaven.
Give us this day our daily bread.
And forgive us our debts,
as we also have forgiven
our debtors.
And do not bring us
to the time of trial,
but rescue us from the evil one.

You Shall Love the Lord

Matthew 22:37-40

In explaining the "greatest commandment" to the scribes, Jesus quotes from the second half of the Shema, a prayer that Jews say every day. It defines the believer's relationship with God and neighbor.

"YOU SHALL LOVE THE LORD YOUR GOD WITH ALL YOUR HEART, AND WITH ALL YOUR SOUL, AND WITH ALL YOUR MIND."

38 THIS IS THE GREATEST AND FIRST COMMANDMENT.

39 AND A SECOND IS LIKE IT: "YOU SHALL LOVE YOUR NEIGHBOR AS YOURSELF."

40 ON THESE TWO COMMANDMENTS HANG ALL THE LAW AND THE PROPHETS."

Hear, O Israel

Mark 12:29-31

In this passage, Jesus prays the Shema, the essential prayer of Judaism. It is a proclamation of the uniqueness of the Lord God and is found in the Old Testament in Deuteronomy 6.

· H · E · A · R ·
ISRAEL
THE LORD
IS OUR GOD
THE LORD ALONE
YOU SHALL
LOVE THE LORD
YOUR GOD
WITH ALL
YOUR HEART
AND WITH ALL
YOUR SOUL
AND WITH ALL
YOUR MIGHT

CANTICLE OF MARY

Luke 1:46-55

As the Mother of God, Mary pours out the wonders of God's plan of salvation in which she has been chosen to participate. The canticle's theme of justice has made it a song of hope for the world's oppressed.

AND MARY *said,*
"My soul magnifies the Lord,
   and my spirit rejoices in God my Savior,
for he has looked with favor on the lowliness of his servant.
   Surely, from now on all generations will call me blessed;
for the Mighty One has done great things for me,
   and holy is his name.
His mercy is for those who fear him
   from generation to generation.
He has shown strength with his arm;
   he has scattered the proud in the thoughts of their hearts.
He has brought down the powerful from their thrones,
   and lifted up the lowly;
he has filled the hungry with good things,
   and sent the rich away empty.
He has helped his servant Israel,
   in remembrance of his mercy,
according to the promise he made to our ancestors,
   to Abraham and to his descendants forever."

"My soul magnifies the Lord,
and my spirit rejoices in God my Savior,
⁴⁸ for he has looked with favor
on the lowliness of his servant.
Surely, from now on all generations
will call me blessed;
⁴⁹ for the Mighty One has done
great things for me,
and holy is his name.
⁵⁰ His mercy is for those who fear him
from generation to generation.
⁵¹ He has shown strength with his arm;
he has scattered the proud
in the thoughts of their hearts.
⁵² He has brought down the
powerful from their thrones
and lifted up the lowly;
⁵³ he has filled the hungry with good things
and sent the rich away empty.
⁵⁴ He has helped his servant Israel,
in remembrance of his mercy,
⁵⁵ according to the promise he
made to our ancestors,
to Abraham & to his descendants forever."

CANTICLE OF ZECHARIAH

Luke 1:68-79

Full of Old Testament imagery and sung by Zechariah, a priest of the Temple, the Canticle of Zechariah underscores how John the Baptist stands with the Old Testament prophets in foretelling the birth of Christ.

BLESSED BE *the Lord God of Israel,*
> *for he has looked favorably on his people and redeemed them.*
He has raised up a mighty savior for us
> *in the house of his servant David,*
as he spoke through the mouth of his holy prophets from of old,
> *that we would be saved from our enemies and from the hand of all who hate us.*
Thus he has shown the mercy promised to our ancestors,
> *and has remembered his holy covenant,*
the oath that he swore

continued on next page

"Blessed be the Lord God of Israel,
for he has looked favorably
    on his people and redeemed them.
⁶⁹ He has raised up a mighty savior for us
    in the house of his servant David,
⁷⁰ as he spoke through the mouth
    of his holy prophets from of old,
⁷¹ that we would be saved from our
    enemies and from the hand
    of all who hate us.
⁷² Thus he has shown the mercy
    promised to our ancestors,
    & has remembered his holy covenant,
⁷³ the oath that he swore

CANTICLE OF ZECHARIAH

Luke 1:68-79

continued from previous page

to our ancestor Abraham,
> *to grant us that we, being rescued from the hands of our enemies,*
might serve him without fear, in holiness and righteousness
> *before him all our days.*
And you, child, will be called the prophet of the Most High;
> *for you will go before the Lord to prepare his ways,*
to give knowledge of salvation to his people
> *by the forgiveness of their sins.*
By the tender mercy of our God,
> *the dawn from on high will break upon us,*
to give light to those who sit in darkness and in the shadow of death,
> *to guide our feet into the way of peace.*

to our ancestor Abraham, to grant us [74] that we, being rescued from the hands of our enemies, might serve him without fear, [75] in holiness & righteousness before him all our days. [76] And you, child, will be called the prophet of the Most High; for you will go before the Lord to prepare his ways, [77] to give knowledge of salvation to his people by the forgiveness of their sins. [78] By the tender mercy of our God, the dawn from on high will break upon us, [79] to give light to those who sit in darkness & in the shadow of death, to guide our feet into the way of peace."

Luke 2:29-32

Both Simeon and Anna confirm Jesus as the fulfillment of Old Testament prophecy. Today the prayer evokes the joy of those who have lived by faith and have seen their hopes realized.

29 "MASTER, NOW YOU ARE
DISMISSING YOUR
SERVANT IN PEACE,
ACCORDING TO YOUR WORD:
30 FOR MY EYES HAVE SEEN
YOUR SALVATION,
31 WHICH YOU HAVE PREPARED
IN THE PRESENCE OF ALL PEOPLES,
32 A LIGHT FOR REVELATION
TO THE GENTILES
AND FOR GLORY TO YOUR
PEOPLE ISRAEL."

You Shall Love the Lord

Luke 10:27

This teaching of Christ is the second half of the Jewish Shema. Its presence in Luke connects the Gentile audience to the promises God has revealed through Jewish people.

LUKE

"YOU SHALL
LOVE THE
LORD YOUR
GOD WITH
ALL YOUR
HEART, AND
WITH ALL
YOUR SOUL,
AND WITH
ALL YOUR
STRENGTH,
AND WITH
ALL YOUR
MIND; & YOUR
NEIGHBOR
AS YOURSELF"

Those Who Believe in Me

John 11:25-26

One of the many passages wherein John the evangelist stresses Christ as the unique Savior of the world.

✝

THOSE WHO
BELIEVE
IN ME EVEN
THOUGH
THEY DIE,
WILL LIVE,
AND
EVERYONE
WHO LIVES
AND BELIEVES
IN ME
WILL NEVER
DIE

Repent and Be Baptized

Acts 2:38

Saint Peter concludes his Pentecost speech with these words of forgiveness and hope. Christ holds out his promise of salvation to all those wanting it.

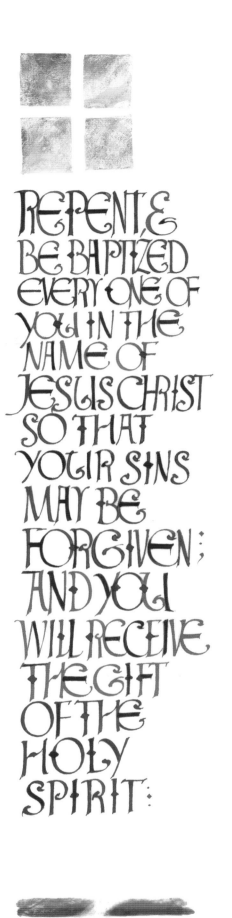

REPENT, &
BE BAPTIZED
EVERY ONE OF
YOU IN THE
NAME OF
JESUS CHRIST
SO THAT
YOUR SINS
MAY BE
FORGIVEN;
AND YOU
WILL RECEIVE
THE GIFT
OF THE
HOLY
SPIRIT:

An exuberant hymn of praise, this psalm invites the faithful to participate in the life-giving wisdom of the Psalter by moving beyond their own concerns and allowing themselves to be caught up in the glory of God.

Psalm 150

Praise the LORD!
Praise God in his sanctuary;
 praise him in his
  mighty firmament!

Praise the LORD!

2 Praise him for his mighty deeds;
 praise him according to
  his surpassing greatness!

3 Praise him with trumpet sound;
 praise him with lute & harp!

4 Praise him with
  tambourine and dance;
 praise him with strings & pipe!

Praise the LORD!

5 Praise him with
  clanging cymbals;
 praise him with
  loud clashing cymbals!

Praise the LORD!

6 Let everything that breathes
 praise the LORD!
Praise the LORD!